SAFETY DOG
DIEGO
GETS ADOPTED

By Angel and Tracey Jimenez

Copyright © 2024
All Rights Reserved
Made in the USA

Dedication

The idea of Safety Dog Diego was inspired by the anticipation of Angel and Tracey becoming grandparents in the spring of 2022. Tracey fondly remembered how her maternal grandmother, Gloria Louise Allen, would create special memories by incorporating Tracey's name and favorite things into some of the books they read together. Inspired by these cherished memories, Tracey wanted to do something similar for her soon-to-be-born grandson, Alexander.

Angel and Tracey realized they already had the perfect concept for a children's book with their French Bulldog named Diego. As a puppy, Diego accompanied Angel, known as the "Safety Guy," on construction site projects and became known as "Safety Dog Diego."

Both Angel and Tracey have a deep love for dogs, having grown up with them, and wanted to share this love with not only their grandson but with all young readers and their families. They are strong advocates for adopting dogs and providing them with loving, forever homes.

About the Authors

Angel and Tracey Jimenez, children's book authors, find inspiration in their experiences raising four children and nurturing their grandson. Along with caring for a variety of pets over the years. With Angel's nearly two decades of expertise as a safety professional, their tales not only captivate young imaginations but also prioritize creating safe and nurturing environments for children to thrive. Along with their faithful family pet, Diego, they seamlessly integrate lessons on child safety into their enchanting narratives, ensuring that young readers gain vital knowledge in a captivating and memorable manner. Through their collective efforts, Angel and Tracey provide a platform for children to learn and grow, guided by a profound commitment to both storytelling and safety.

In the vibrant city of San Diego, a lively and curious French Bulldog puppy named Diego found his home. With his bright, round eyes gleaming, Diego eagerly trotted through the sunny streets. He was ready to explore every corner of his bustling neighborhood. This is Diego's story.

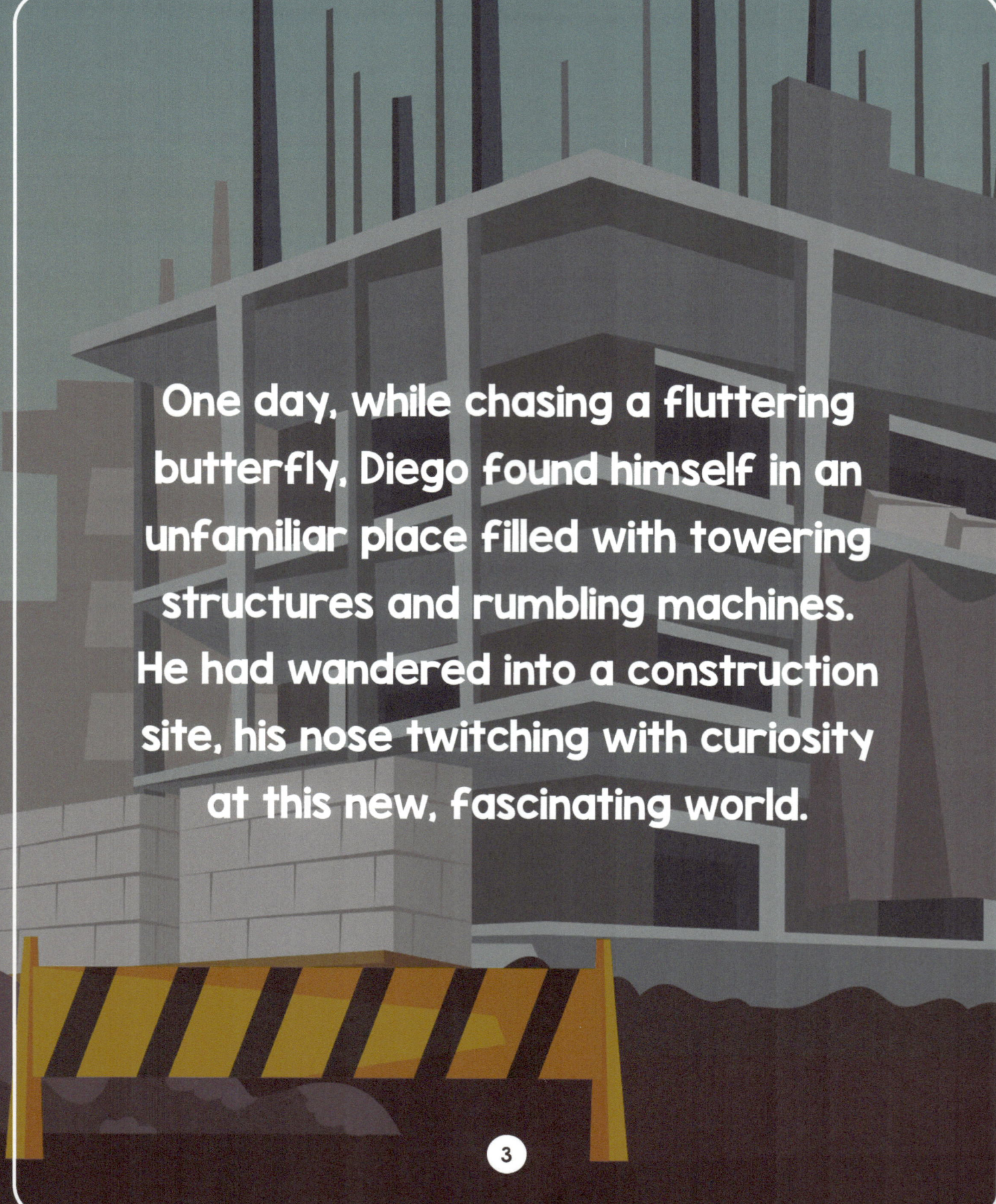

One day, while chasing a fluttering butterfly, Diego found himself in an unfamiliar place filled with towering structures and rumbling machines. He had wandered into a construction site, his nose twitching with curiosity at this new, fascinating world.

As Diego sniffed around, he climbed into the bucket of a bulldozer. Suddenly, he heard a friendly voice. It was the Safety Guy, who gently lifted Diego out and wrapped him in a bright yellow safety vest.

"You must be careful here, little one," he said with a smile.

Back in the office, the Safety Guy called his wife, Mimi. "I found this little guy at the site. Can we keep him until we find his home?" Mimi agreed, with one condition: Diego must accompany the Safety Guy to work, as no one was home during the day to watch him.

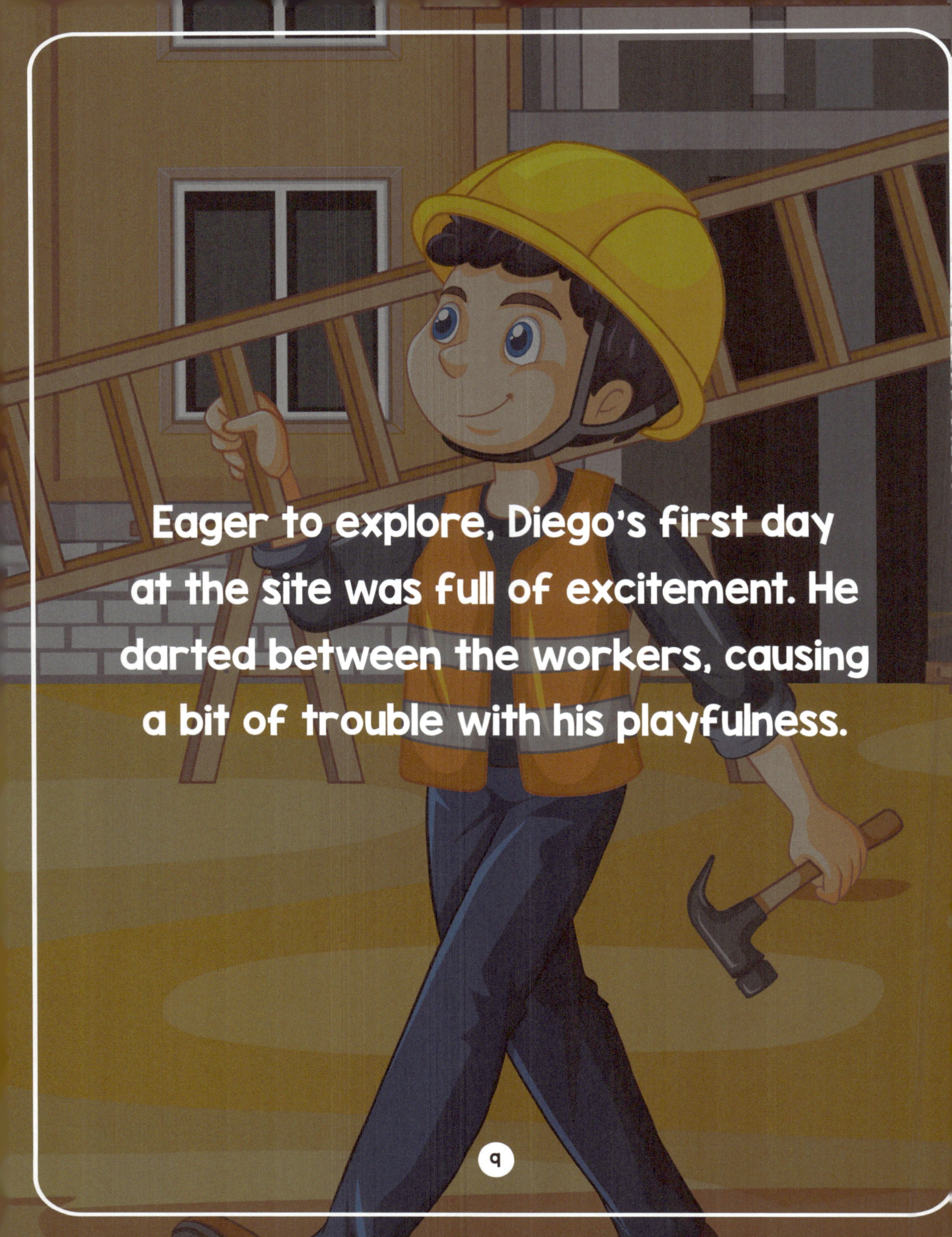

Eager to explore, Diego's first day at the site was full of excitement. He darted between the workers, causing a bit of trouble with his playfulness.

The Safety Guy sat down with Diego, teaching him the importance of safety and attention at the construction site. He even gave Diego his own little hard hat and safety vest, making him an honorary member of the team.

Trying to be part of the team, Diego attempted to help a worker carry some tools. But, oops! He accidentally knocked over the tool box, feeling a bit down about his mistake.

The Safety Guy knelt beside Diego, reassuring him with kind words. "Mistakes help us learn, Diego. You're doing great!" It's important to "Stay Safe and Stay Well!"

Inspired by the Safety Guy's words, Diego became more observant. He noticed a worker gearing up and fetched his safety goggles for him.

One day, Diego's sharp eyes caught sight of a loose guardrail on a rooftop. He barked and pointed with his nose, alerting the workers to the danger.

Touched by Diego's dedication, Mimi and the Safety Guy decided to officially adopt him. "You're part of our family now, Diego," they said, giving him a warm, loving home.

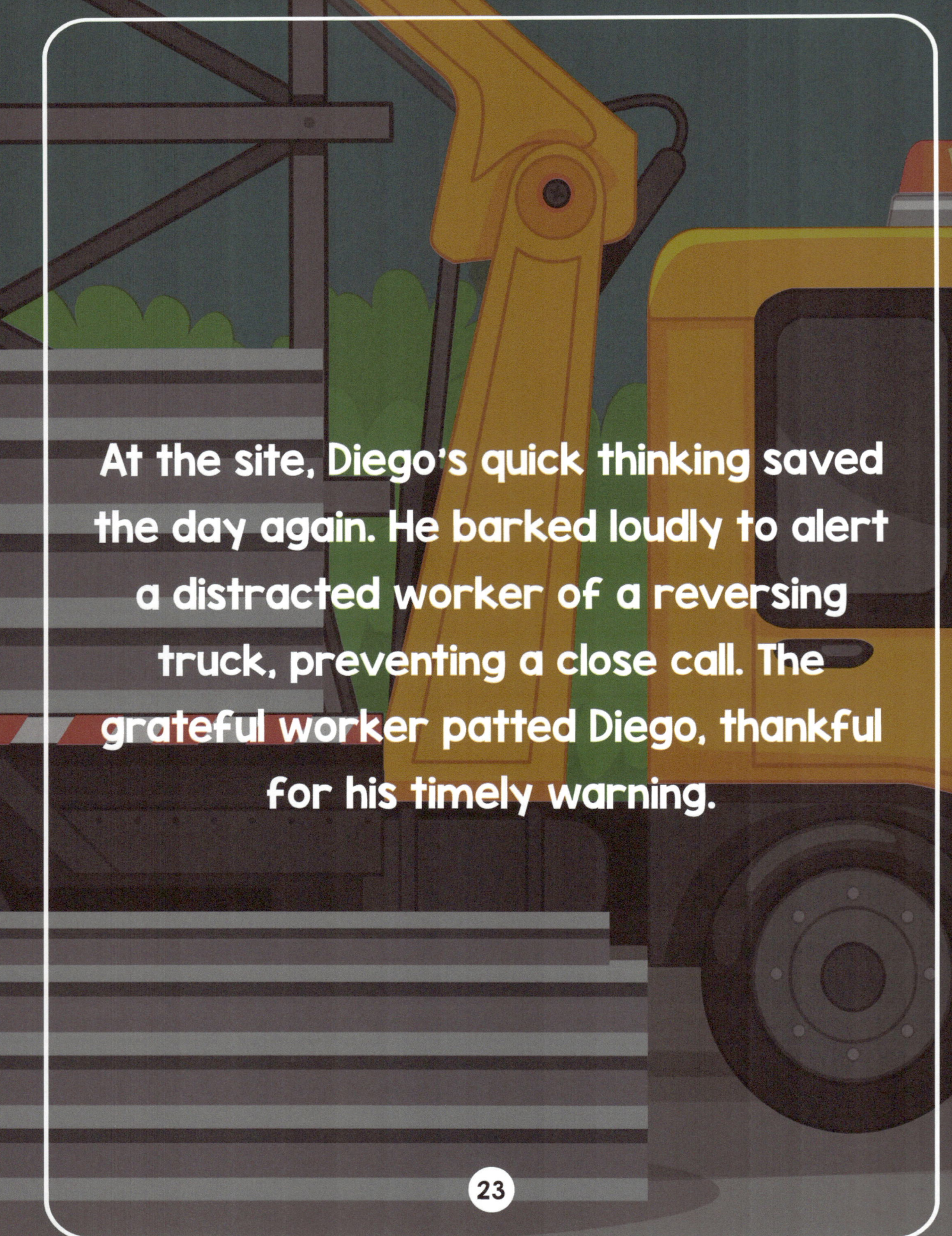

At the site, Diego's quick thinking saved the day again. He barked loudly to alert a distracted worker of a reversing truck, preventing a close call. The grateful worker patted Diego, thankful for his timely warning.

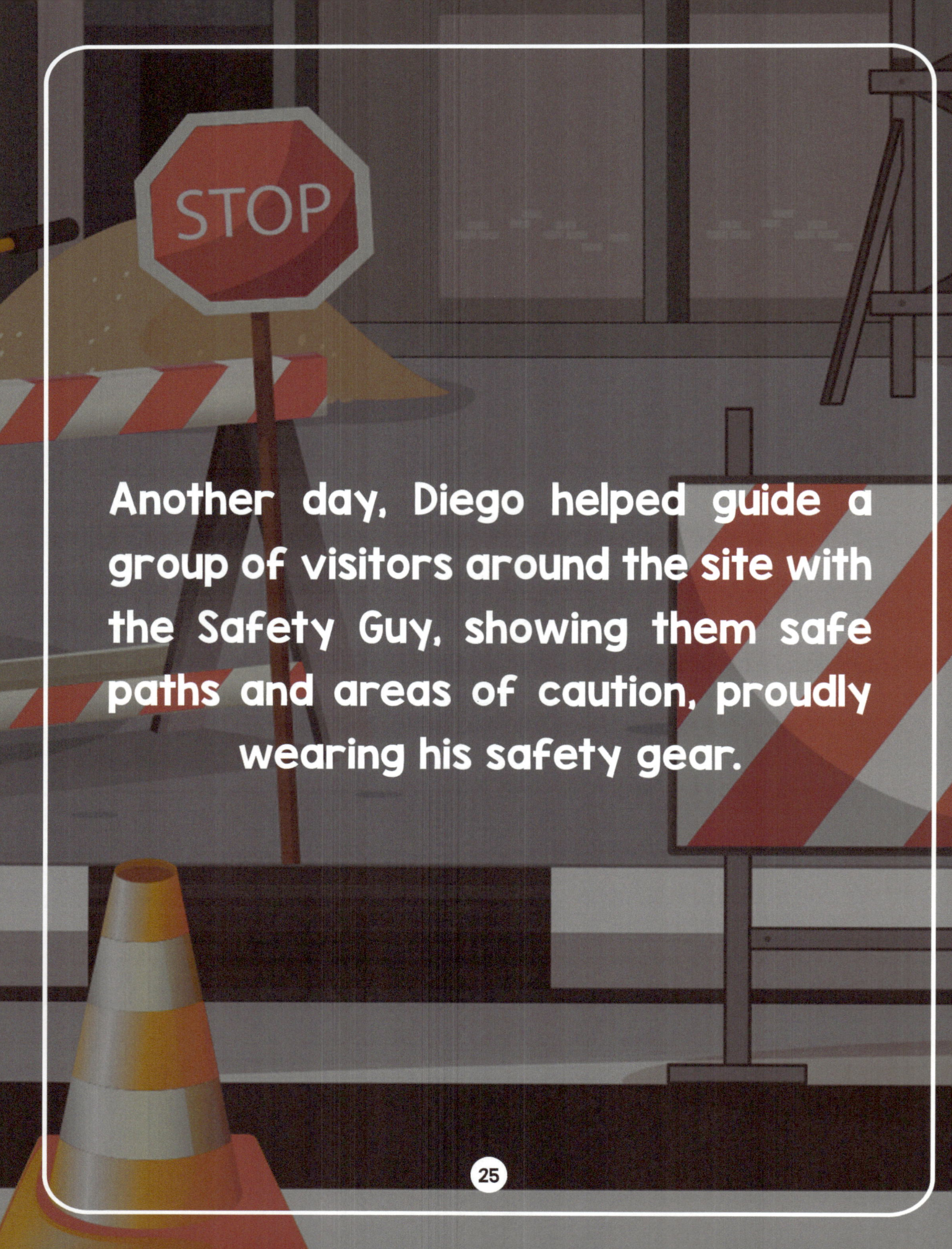

Another day, Diego helped guide a group of visitors around the site with the Safety Guy, showing them safe paths and areas of caution, proudly wearing his safety gear.

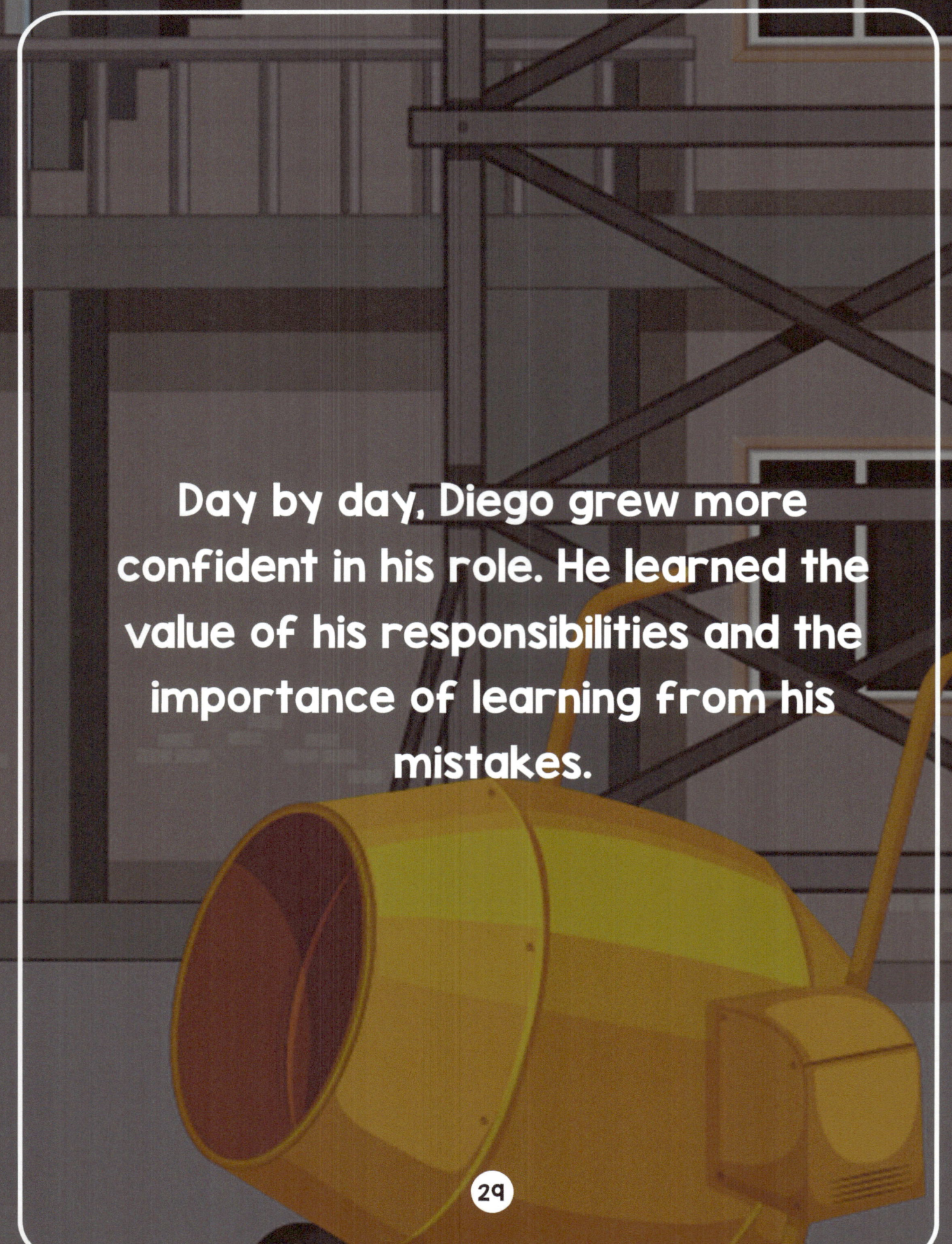

Day by day, Diego grew more confident in his role. He learned the value of his responsibilities and the importance of learning from his mistakes.

One day, the workers gave Diego a special gift: an honorary Safety Officer Certificate. In a ceremony filled with smiles and cheers, Diego proudly wore his personalized safety gear: a vest, hard hat, and goggles.

Standing next to the Safety Guy, Diego's eyes sparkled with pride. He had found a purpose at the construction site, reminding everyone of the importance of safety. Every night, he snuggled up with his new family, dreaming of tomorrow's adventures.

With a heart full of bravery and a nose for safety, Diego was more than a pup - he was a hero, leaving paw prints of love and safety wherever he went.

The end.

Safety Dog Diego (Theme Song)

Safety Dog Diego
Safety Dog Diego
Safety Dog Diego
He's the ONE! ONE! ONE!

Safety Dog Diego
Safety Dog Diego
Safety Dog Diego
So much FUN! FUN! FUN!

He's brown and tan and shakes his tail,
He says "STAY SAFE AND STAY WELL!"

Safety Dog Diego
Safety Dog Diego
Safety Dog Diego
He's the ONE! ONE! ONE!

Safety Oath

I promise to be safe each day,
In all my work and all my play.
I'll wear my gear and take it slow,
Safety first, that's how I'll grow.

I promise to be safe and kind.
To always keep safety in mind.
I'll wear my helmet and buckle up tight, and make sure I'm seen in the day or night.

I'll look both ways when crossing the street, and make sure my surroundings are always neat.

I'll listen, think, and do things swell.
So I can Stay Safe and Stay Well!

Milton Keynes UK
Ingram Content Group UK Ltd.
UKHW050749141124
451207UK00001B/16